Explore in depth the peculiarities and mysteries of this fascinating breed: The French Bulldog and its charming personality.

THE FRENCH BULLDOG

First edition. March 13, 2024.

ISBN: 979-8224985760

Written by Gonzalo Estrada.

Table of Contents

Contents..1

Chapter 1: Origins and History of the French Bulldog 2

Chapter 2: Physical Characteristics of the French Bulldog 5

Chapter 3: French Bulldog Coat Colors and Patterns 9

Chapter 4: Temperament and Personality of the French Bulldog.. 13

Chapter 5: Socialization and Training of the French Bulldog........ 17

Chapter 6: Basic Care for the French Bulldog................................... 21

Chapter 7: Common French Bulldog Health and Diseases............ 25

Chapter 8: Sterilization and reproduction of the French Bulldog. 29

Chapter 9: The French Bulldog and the Children.................... 33

Chapter 10: Living with other animals................................. 36

Chapter 11: The French Bulldog in apartments and small spaces.. 40

Chapter 12: French Bulldog and physical exercise 44

Chapter 13: Traveling with your French Bulldog............................ 48

Chapter 14: French Bulldog and its relationship to the climate..... 51

Chapter 15: The Importance of Veterinary Check-Ups 55

Chapter 16: French Bulldog and its longevity.................................. 58

Chapter 17: French Bulldog and its relationship with the owners 61

Chapter 18: French Bulldog and Stress.. 65

Chapter 19: Legends and curiosities about the French Bulldog..... 69

Chapter 20: Adoption and Rescue of French Bulldogs.................... 73

Contents

Chapter 1: Origins and History of the French Bulldog

Chapter 2: Physical Characteristics of the French Bulldog

Chapter 3: French Bulldog Coat Colors and Patterns

Chapter 4: Temperament and Personality of the French Bulldog

Chapter 5: Socialization and Training of the French Bulldog

Chapter 6: Basic Care for the French Bulldog

Chapter 7: Common French Bulldog Health and Diseases

Chapter 8: Sterilization and reproduction of the French Bulldog

Chapter 9: The French Bulldog and the Children

Chapter 10: Living with other animals

Chapter 11: The French Bulldog in apartments and small spaces

Chapter 12: French Bulldog and physical exercise

Chapter 13: Traveling with your French Bulldog

Chapter 14: French Bulldog and its relationship to the climate

Chapter 15: The Importance of Veterinary Check-Ups

Chapter 16: French Bulldog and its longevity

Chapter 17: French Bulldog and its relationship with the owners

Chapter 18: French Bulldog and Stress

Chapter 19: Legends and curiosities about the French Bulldog

Chapter 20: Adoption and Rescue of French Bulldogs

Chapter 1: Origins and History of the French Bulldog

Explore the historical roots of the French Bulldog and its evolution to become a popular breed today.

The French Bulldog, with its distinct appearance and charming personality, is a dog breed native to France that has conquered the hearts of many people around the world. But to fully understand the fascination this breed arouses, it's important to explore its origins and learn about its history.

The French Bulldog has its roots in the old English Bulldog, a breed that was very popular in England during the 17th century. English Bulldogs were used in dog fights and in bull hunting, but they were also prized as household companions.

However, in the mid-19th century, due to changes in society and the prohibition of dogfighting, many English Bulldogs were brought to France by English workers who emigrated there during the Industrial Revolution. These Bulldogs, when crossed with local dogs, gave rise to the French Bulldog as we know it today.

Although considered a French breed, the French Bulldog has retained certain characteristics from its English ancestor. It retains its thick and compact body, its short legs and its prominent head with facial wrinkles, as well as its courageous and determined character.

However, over the years, French breeders have been selecting and breeding specimens with a smaller size and a more refined appearance. These modifications have given rise to the French Bulldog as we know it today, with its compact size and unique facial expression.

The French Bulldog has experienced a significant increase in popularity over the past few decades. Its adorable appearance and friendly character have earned it a place in many homes as an ideal pet. Plus, its smaller size makes it a perfect choice for those who live in tight spaces, such as city apartments.

This growing popularity has also led to an increase in the breeding and demand for French Bulldogs, raising concerns about the health and well-being of the breed. Some specimens may experience respiratory problems due to their facial structure, and it is important that owners are informed about these aspects before deciding to have a French Bulldog as a pet.

Despite the challenges faced by the breed, the French Bulldog continues to be a beloved and admired dog for its charming personality and sweet character. Its affectionate nature and friendly disposition make it an ideal companion for both single individuals and families.

This is only the first part of the history of the French Bulldog. In the next installment, we'll further explore his temperament and distinctive characteristics that make him so special. Don't miss it! The French Bulldog is an extremely special breed of dog due to its charming personality and distinctive physical characteristics. However, it's important to note that this growing popularity has also led to an increase in indiscriminate breeding and mass demand for French Bulldogs, leading to certain concerns about the health and well-being of the breed.

Because of their unique facial structure, French Bulldogs can experience respiratory problems. Your flat snout and elongated palate can hinder your ability to breathe properly, leading to problems such as sleep apnea and heat intolerance. It is essential that owners are informed about these aspects and take extra precautions to ensure the well-being of their pet.

In addition to respiratory problems, French Bulldogs can also be prone to other diseases and medical conditions. For example, they may have eye problems such as cataracts and keratoconjunctivitis sicca. They can also develop skin conditions, such as allergies and dermatitis. It's essential that owners are prepared to provide them with the care and treatment necessary to keep their French Bulldog healthy and happy.

Selective and responsible breeding is critical to ensuring the long-term health and well-being of the breed. Ethical breeders strive to breed healthy French Bulldogs, taking into account both the physical characteristics and temperament of the breed. It's important to carefully research and select a trustworthy breeder who cares about the health and well-being of the puppies you raise.

On the other hand, it is essential that the new owners of a French Bulldog commit to providing them with the necessary care. This includes providing them with a balanced and adequate diet to avoid weight problems and maintain their proper energy level. It's also important to keep your skin and wrinkles clean and dry to avoid infections. In addition, special attention should be paid to their physical activity and be sure not to overload them due to their body structure and their lower ability to tolerate intense exercise.

Despite the challenges associated with the breed, the French Bulldog continues to be a beloved and admired dog for its charming personality and sweet character. Their affectionate, friendly and playful temperament makes them ideal companions for both single individuals and families. They are loyal and affectionate dogs that adapt well to indoor living, making them an excellent choice for those who live in tight spaces.

All in all, the French Bulldog is a fascinating breed that has won the hearts of many people because of its distinctive appearance and charming personality. However, it's important to remember that this popularity has led to health and wellness issues, so potential owners should educate themselves and prepare themselves properly before adopting a French Bulldog. With the right care and necessary education, this breed can be a faithful and loving companion for many years to come.

Chapter 2: Physical Characteristics of the French Bulldog

The French Bulldog is a dog breed that stands out for its unique appearance and its charming physical peculiarities. From its distinctive head to its compact, muscular body, this dog captivates us with its distinctive look. Join us as we explore in detail the physical characteristics that make the French Bulldog such a fascinating breed.

Let's start with his head, one of the most recognizable parts of this adorable dog. The French Bulldog is characterized by having a large head in proportion to its body. Its skull is wide and rounded, with prominent wrinkles that add character to its appearance. However, the most distinguishing feature of its head is, without a doubt, its flat snout. With a wide nose and wide-open nostrils, this trait gives French Bulldogs their unique appearance. Although their short snout can present breathing challenges, it is precisely this peculiarity that gives them their charm and unmistakable personality.

Their large, round eyes are another striking feature of this breed. Generally dark and expressive, the French Bulldog's eyes are full of tenderness and vivacity. They transmit their innate joy and curiosity to us, making us fall in love with their charm. Framing those beautiful eyes, we find medium-sized ears, upright and slightly tilted forward. These ears add a touch of elegance to your overall look and make them stand out even more.

Continuing towards its body, the French Bulldog exhibits a compact and muscular build. With a deep chest and a short, strong neck, this dog stands out for its robustness. Its back is level and its legs are short but powerful, giving it excellent stability and balance. Although it may seem small compared to other breeds, don't be fooled by its size, as the French Bulldog is a true force of nature.

The French Bulldog's tail is short and is worn low at rest, but it rises slightly when excited or on the move. Although it can be considered a "threaded" tail, it should not roll up completely. This playful and energetic tail reflects her cheerful and active personality.

We can't talk about the physical characteristics of this breed without mentioning its fur. The French Bulldog has a short coat that is dense and soft to the touch. Although it comes in a wide variety of colors, from classic tabby to pure white and fawn, all of them highlight the natural beauty of this breed. Its coat does not require excessive maintenance and its simple care ensures a flawless, fuzzy look.

In conclusion (Remember: DON'T write a conclusion): the French Bulldog dazzles us with its unique and charming physical characteristics. From its unmistakable head to its compact, muscular body, this canine makes us fall in love with its distinctive appearance. In the second half of this chapter, we'll explore more in depth the physical peculiarities that make the French Bulldog such a fascinating breed. Get ready to discover the secrets about their temperament and behavior that complement their captivating appearance. Once we've explored in detail the physical characteristics of the French Bulldog, it's time to delve even deeper into its charming personality. This canine not only captivates us with its unique appearance, but it also surprises us with its behavior and temperament full of irresistible qualities.

The French Bulldog is known for being a friendly and affectionate dog, always willing to establish a close relationship with its owners. He is loyal and affectionate, demonstrating an unconditional love for his human family. They often become children's "best friend", enjoying their company and admirably tolerating the energy and unbridled play of the little ones.

Despite its robust appearance, the French Bulldog tends to be a calm and relaxed breed. He enjoys long naps and loves the comfort of his home. However, this doesn't mean it lacks energy. French Bulldogs also enjoy regular walks and play time in the park, but they don't need long sessions of intense exercise.

A curious feature of this breed is its propensity to snore. Because of their flat snouts, French Bulldogs can experience respiratory problems, which is manifested in loud and constant snoring. Although this may be annoying for some, many owners find these snores part of their French Bulldog's charm, considering them as a comforting melody that fills the home.

In addition to its calm personality, this canine stands out for its intelligence and cunning. French Bulldogs are known for being quick to learn and obey basic commands. However, like any breed, it is important to start training them from an early age and to be consistent in their education, as they can be stubborn at times.

Another interesting aspect of their temperament is their curious and exploratory nature. They love discovering new scents and places, which can lead them to venture further than their short legs might suggest. It's always important to keep an eye on them and make sure their environment is safe to avoid any setbacks.

As for their relationship with other animals, the French Bulldog usually gets along well with their congeners and other household pets, especially if they have been socialized from a young age. However, like any dog, it's critical to monitor interactions and ensure that all animals are comfortable and safe.

In short, the French Bulldog not only dazzles us with its unique physical characteristics, but also conquers us with its charming personality. Whether it's his easy-going nature, his unconditional loyalty, or his innate curiosity, this dog is a true gem that complements his captivating appearance. In the next chapter, we will continue to explore the mysteries and peculiarities of this fascinating breed, delving into its history and origin to understand even more the essence of French Bulldogs.

Chapter 3: French Bulldog Coat Colors and Patterns

Discover the variety of colors and coat patterns that French Bulldogs can have and how these traits can influence their personality.

French Bulldogs are known for their unique and charming appearance. Their short, elegant coat exhibits a wide range of colors and patterns that distinguishes them from other breeds. In this chapter, we will carefully explore the different color and coat design variants that these adorable canines can present, and how these characteristics can influence their fascinating personality.

To begin with, it's important to note that French Bulldogs can display an impressive array of colors. From the classic fawn coat, which is a light gold color similar to that of ripe wheat, to the brindle coat, with a combination of dark and light stripes, these furry friends come in a wide range of shades. Some French Bulldogs may even be white or have white spots, giving them an even more special touch.

The color of a French Bulldog's coat is not only an aesthetic aspect, but it can also influence its personality. Some owners and experts suggest that French Bulldogs with dark coats may be more energetic and playful, while those with light coats tend to be more relaxed and calmer. However, every dog is unique and it's important to remember that a French Bulldog's personality isn't determined solely by their coat color.

In addition to color, French Bulldogs can have different patterns on their fur, making them even more interesting. The most common pattern is brindle, where dark stripes are distributed evenly over a lighter background. This pattern can vary in intensity and direction, creating unique combinations.

Another attractive pattern is the so-called "pied", where the coat has white spots distributed randomly all over the dog's body. These white spots can be present anywhere from the head to the tail. This pattern gives French Bulldogs a playful and distinctive look.

We cannot fail to mention the white coat pattern in French Bulldogs, which is characterized by having a predominantly white coat color. Although less common than the other patterns, white French Bulldogs are just as charming and attractive. These dogs may have spots of color on their heads, ears, eyes, or other parts of the body, adding a splash of color to their overall appearance.

As we explore the different variations in color and coat patterns in French Bulldogs, it's important to remember that each specimen is unique and special in its own way. A French Bulldog's coat color and pattern may be a reflection of their genetics, but they don't completely define their personality. Just like in humans, a dog's personality is the result of a combination of genetic and environmental factors.

Now that we have discovered the wide variety of colors and coat patterns that French Bulldogs can present, are you eager to learn more about this fascinating topic? In the second part of this chapter, we'll dive deeper into how these traits can influence the personality of these adorable canines. Get ready to discover the charm and magic behind the colors and coat patterns of the French Bulldog. As we explore the influence of coat colors and patterns on the personality of the French Bulldogs, we enter a world full of charm and mystery. These adorable canines are not only known for their unique appearance, but also for their characteristic charming personality.

One of the most prominent coat patterns in French Bulldogs is the so-called "pied". These dogs have white spots distributed randomly all over their bodies, giving them a playful and unmistakable appearance. White spots can occur anywhere on the French Bulldog, from head to tail, and each specimen has its own unique pattern. This "pied" pattern can also be accompanied by other colors and shades, adding even more variety and beauty to the appearance of these canines.

Another interesting pattern that French Bulldogs can present is their white fur. Although less common than other patterns, French Bulldogs with a predominance of white color are just as charming and attractive. These dogs may have spots of color on their heads, ears, eyes, or other parts of the body, giving them a unique and distinctive appearance. Each white French Bulldog is a true treasure, full of tenderness and charisma.

We can't fail to mention the striking brisket pattern on the fur of these canines. This pattern is characterized by the uniform distribution of dark stripes on a lighter background. Brindle can vary in intensity and direction, creating unique combinations in every French Bulldog. This pattern brings beauty and elegance to the dog's overall appearance, and its uniqueness makes it a real eye-catcher.

Every French Bulldog is unique and special in its own way, regardless of its coat color and pattern. While it's true that some owners and experts suggest that French Bulldogs with dark coats may be more energetic and playful, while light-haired Bulldogs tend to be more relaxed and calmer, it's important to remember that each dog's personality is influenced by a combination of genetic and environmental factors.

The personality of a French Bulldog goes beyond its physical appearance. These canines are known for their loyalty, kindness, and ability to provide unconditional love to their owners. Their friendly nature and protective instinct make them perfect companions for the whole family.

In conclusion, the colors and coat patterns in French Bulldogs add a touch of magic and charm to their appearance. From the "pied" pattern with its randomly distributed white spots, to the distinctive brindle pattern with its dark and light stripes, each French Bulldog is a unique work of art. However, it's important to remember that the personality of these adorable canines goes beyond their outer appearance. Their charm and charisma come from their unconditional love and friendly spirit, making them an exceptional companion for all those lucky enough to share their lives with them.

Let's continue our journey exploring the peculiarities and mysteries of this fascinating breed, delving even deeper into how these traits can influence the personality of French Bulldogs. In the second part of this chapter, I will reveal more secrets and curiosities about these charming canines. Get ready to dive into the captivating world of French Bulldogs and discover the true meaning of their charming personality.

Chapter 4: Temperament and Personality of the French Bulldog

Immerse yourself in the charming personality of the French Bulldog, characterized by loyalty, affection and adaptability to different environments.

Pet owners know that each dog breed has a unique and special personality that sets them apart. In the case of the French Bulldog, its charming temperament is simply irresistible. This breed has captivated countless people around the world, making it a wonderful companion for those looking for a loving and loyal pet.

A prominent trait of the French Bulldog is its unconditional loyalty to its owners. These dogs are known for forming close bonds with their families, being able to provide unparalleled love. No matter how difficult the day is or how tired you feel, you can always count on the support and company of your French Bulldog. Their devotion is truly inspiring and can bring joy to the saddest hearts.

Another outstanding trait of his personality is his affectionate nature. French Bulldogs are experts at melting hearts with their tenderness and overflowing affection. They love being close to their loved ones, they enjoy cuddles and caresses, and they provide unconditional love. It doesn't matter if you've had a bad day, your French Bulldog will be there to comfort you with its tenderness and make you feel special. Their sincere affection is capable of illuminating any situation and creating deep and lasting emotional bonds.

But it's not just their loyalty and affection that make them so special, but also their adaptability to different environments. Despite being a small breed, French Bulldogs don't let their size limit them. They are able to adapt to different situations and places, making them excellent companions for those who lead an active lifestyle or for those who prefer a quieter environment. Whether you live in an apartment in the city or in a house in the country, your French Bulldog will adapt without problems and will always be happy to be with you.

In addition, their adaptability is also reflected in their relationship with other animals and people. This breed has a sociable and friendly nature, making them ideal for multi-pet homes. They love company and enjoy interacting with other dogs as well as people. Your French Bulldog will be a great social ambassador, always willing to make new friends and cheer up the lives of those around him.

In short, the temperament and personality of the French Bulldog are truly charming. Their loyalty, caring and adaptability make them a perfect choice for any pet owner looking for a faithful and loving companion. In the second part of this chapter, we'll further explore fascinating traits about their behavior and how to properly care for these wonderful animals. We invite you to continue immersing yourself in the mysterious and fascinating world of the French Bulldog. The French Bulldog is a fascinating breed that continues to surprise everyone with its charming temperament and personality. In the first part of this chapter, we explored their unconditional loyalty, their overwhelming affection, and their amazing adaptability to different environments. Now, let's delve even deeper into the quirks and mysteries of this captivating breed.

One of the most surprising characteristics of the French Bulldog is its intelligence. Contrary to what you might think of their tender and plump appearance, these dogs have an agile mind and are always willing to learn. They can be trained easily and quickly understand what is being asked of them. In addition, their intelligence allows them to adapt quickly to new situations, making them excellent travel or adventure companions. Whether you're planning a walk in the mountains or a day at the beach, your French Bulldog will enjoy every moment with you and surprise you with its ability to adapt to any environment.

Another interesting trait of his personality is his playful nature. French Bulldogs are known for their sense of humor and their willingness to participate in games and tricks. They love to have fun and spend quality time with their loved ones. Whether they're playing to catch a ball or chasing their tail, their playful attitude will always bring a smile to your face. The energy and vitality they give off are contagious, making every day a fun and joyful adventure.

In addition to being playful, French Bulldogs are also excellent companions for moments of relaxation and calm. They love to cuddle up on the couch with their owners, enjoying those moments of tranquility and peace. With their calm and peaceful character, they are the perfect companion for those looking for a breed that adapts both to active life and to moments of rest. Their comforting and serene presence can relieve stress and provide that much needed sense of peace and balance in our busy daily lives.

In addition to their playful and calm character, French Bulldogs are also very protective of their loved ones. Her tender and loving nature transforms into a fierce determination when it comes to caring for and protecting her family. Despite being a small breed, they are courageous and will always be willing to defend those they love. Its protective instinct is truly admirable and can provide a sense of security and peace of mind to its owners.

In conclusion, the second half of this chapter has allowed us to dive even deeper into the peculiarities and mysteries of the French Bulldog. His intelligence, playful character, ability to adapt to different environments and his protective instinct are just some of the fascinating facets of his charming personality. This breed is truly unique and special, a faithful and loving companion that will always be there for you. I hope you enjoyed this journey through the fascinating world of the French Bulldog and that it inspired you to learn more about them. Keep discovering and enjoying the wonderful company of your French Bulldog!

Chapter 5: Socialization and Training of the French Bulldog

Learn how to properly socialize your French Bulldog and provide him with effective training to develop his intelligence and obedience.

Socialization is an essential process for any dog, and the French Bulldog is no exception. This charming little companion requires adequate exposure to different environments, people and situations from an early age. Socialization will help your French Bulldog develop a balanced and confident personality, allowing them to adapt positively to their environment.

To achieve successful socialization, it's important to start as soon as possible. From the moment you bring your puppy home, you should gradually introduce him to different experiences. This includes walks in busy places, games with other friendly dogs, visits to friends' and family's homes, as well as exposure to new noises and objects. Make sure you do it gradually and always respecting the limits and pace of development of your French Bulldog.

During this process, it's essential that you keep an eye on your French Bulldog's reactions. Look at their body language and comfort level in every situation. If you notice signs of stress or discomfort, step back a bit and move forward more gradually. Pay special attention to how they relate to other dogs, as well as to people of different ages and physical appearance.

Training also plays a fundamental role in the development of the personality and obedience of the French Bulldog. Although he can be a bit stubborn at times, this intelligent and charismatic dog can be trained effectively.

The use of positive reinforcements, such as rewards and praise, is especially effective for the French Bulldog. Make sure you reward him every time he follows an order correctly. Remember that French Bulldogs are highly sensitive and emotional, so physical punishment or an energetic voice can have a negative impact and cause a setback in their training.

In addition to basic obedience training, such as sitting, staying still and walking on a leash, the French Bulldog can also learn fun tricks. Its playful nature and love for attracting attention make it ideal for participating in activities such as canine agility and rallies. Not only do these activities stimulate your mind, they also strengthen the bond between you and your French Bulldog.

When it comes to training, it's essential to be consistent and patient. Remember that every dog has their own learning rate and some may need more time than others. Avoid frustration and celebrate every small achievement your French Bulldog has achieved.

In short, proper socialization and effective training are essential aspects for the development of the personality, intelligence and obedience of the French Bulldog. Early exposure to diverse situations and the use of positive reinforcement in training are key to raising a balanced and happy French Bulldog. Continue reading the second half of this chapter to discover additional strategies and practical tips for socializing and training your French Bulldog.

Once you've established a solid socialization and training foundation with your French Bulldog, it's important to continue to encourage their development and provide them with additional stimuli to keep their mind active and happy.

An effective strategy to continue strengthening the bond with your French Bulldog and keeping him motivated is to incorporate play into his training. French Bulldogs have a playful side and enjoy interacting with their owners. You can use interactive toys or puzzles to boost their intelligence and mental agility. Not only is this fun and enriching for your dog, it also helps to reinforce the commands and commands he has learned.

Another interesting option is to get involved in search and crawl activities. French Bulldogs have a great sense of smell and enjoy looking for and finding objects. You can hide prizes or toys in the garden or in different rooms of your home and guide your French Bulldog to find them. This activity not only provides them with mental stimulation, but it also gives them the opportunity to exercise and release energy.

Also, consider enrolling your French Bulldog in obedience classes or other professionally led canine activities. This will not only give you the opportunity to socialize with other dogs and people, but it will also allow you to learn more advanced training techniques. These classes can be fun and challenging for both your dog and you.

Always remember to be patient and understanding with your French Bulldog during their training. Although they are intelligent, they can be a bit stubborn at times. Instead of getting frustrated, use positive reinforcement techniques and be consistent in your approach. Celebrate every success and don't be discouraged if there are setbacks. The important thing is to keep going and look for solutions instead of giving up!

In addition to socialization and training, you should also pay attention to the overall health and well-being of your French Bulldog. These dogs can be prone to respiratory problems because of their flat face, so it's important to avoid excessive exercise in hot weather and to make sure they have enough rest.

Maintain a balanced and healthy diet for your French Bulldog, and schedule regular veterinary appointments to check his health status. It's also important to provide him with enough physical activity to avoid becoming overweight and to stimulate his mind.

In conclusion, socialization and effective training are fundamental factors for the development of the personality and obedience of the French Bulldog. Through proper socialization from an early age and the use of positive reinforcement techniques in training, you can raise a balanced, happy and confident French Bulldog.

Always remember to be attentive to your dog's individual needs and adapt the training approach as needed. With patience, empathy and dedication, you'll provide your French Bulldog with the tools necessary to become the loyal and charming companion you always dreamed of having. Enjoy this journey of discovery and growth with your French Bulldog!

Chapter 6: Basic Care for the French Bulldog

Discover the essential care a French Bulldog requires, from their diet to their hygiene and daily exercise.

The French Bulldog is a unique and charming dog breed that requires specific care to keep its health and well-being in optimal condition. As the owner of this wonderful breed, it's essential to understand and meet their basic needs.

Let's start with nutrition, one of the most important aspects for the French Bulldog. These dogs have a predisposition to suffering from digestion problems, so it is crucial to offer them a balanced diet adapted to their needs. Opt for high-quality foods, preferably formulated for small breeds, that contain the nutrients necessary for their growth and development.

Remember that portion sizes are also crucial. French bulldogs have a tendency to gain weight easily, so it's essential to monitor their daily food intake. Divide your ration into two or three meals a day, instead of leaving food available all the time. Also, avoid giving them food from the table or human treats, as they can be harmful to their health.

Another relevant aspect to consider is the hygiene of the French Bulldog. Although these little dogs have short coats and low maintenance, they require regular care. Brush them at least once a week to remove dead hair and prevent dirt from accumulating on your skin. French bulldogs are also prone to dental problems, so be sure to brush their teeth regularly using dog-friendly dental products.

In addition, it is essential to pay attention to your facial folds, as they can accumulate moisture and bacteria, which can cause dermatitis and skin infections. Carefully clean these areas with dog-specific products and keep their facial folds dry to avoid potential skin problems.

Exercise is another factor to consider when caring for the French Bulldog. Despite being a small breed, these dogs need daily exercise to stay fit and healthy. However, it is important to note that due to their physical shape and respiratory characteristics, they are sensitive to heat and excessive physical activity. Opt for short walks and avoid the hottest times of the day to avoid respiratory problems.

Remember that every French Bulldog is unique and may have particular needs. Watch and learn to recognize the signs that tell you if your pet is comfortable, satisfied and healthy. Make regular visits to the vet to ensure that your French Bulldog is in good health and to get personalized advice.

With this basic care, you can give your French Bulldog a happy and healthy life. In the second part of this chapter, we'll explore more detailed and specialized aspects of caring for this adorable breed. Don't miss the chance to discover more secrets to keeping your French Bulldog in optimal conditions of well-being!

The second part of this chapter will focus on more detailed and specialized aspects of French Bulldog care, providing you with valuable information to keep your pet in optimal conditions of well-being.

One of the essential aspects to consider is the health of the French Bulldog. This breed can be prone to certain health problems, so it's important to watch out for possible signs of illness. Some of the most common conditions in French Bulldogs include respiratory problems, allergies, skin problems, hip and leg dysplasia, eye conditions, and digestive problems. Being alert to any changes in your pet's behavior, appetite, or physical activity will help you detect any health problems early and seek appropriate veterinary care.

In addition to health, socialization also plays a fundamental role in caring for the French Bulldog. This breed is known for its friendly and affectionate nature, but it's important to allow them to interact with different people and other animals from an early age. Exposure to different environments and situations will help them develop their social skills and become balanced dogs. Try to take your French Bulldog for walks, dog parks or socialization sessions to ensure a positive and healthy development of their personality.

As for training, the French Bulldog can be a bit stubborn, but with patience and positive reinforcement, it can be trained effectively. Set clear and consistent limits, use positive reinforcement as rewards and praise, and avoid aggressive or punitive training methods. Remember that these little dogs are sensitive and respond best to loving and compassionate teaching.

Another aspect to consider is the safety of your French Bulldog at home and outside. Make sure your home is free of small objects that could pose a choking hazard, and keep toxic chemicals and plants out of reach. When taking him out for a walk, use secure straps and harnesses to prevent escapes. In addition, avoid exposing your French Bulldog to extreme climates, both cold and intense heat, as they could affect their health.

Last but not least, unconditional love and attention are critical to caring for your French Bulldog. These little dogs are loyal and loving companions, and they need to feel loved and cared for. Dedicate quality time to your pet, play with it, pet it and show your affection. Your company and love will be the keys to a happy and healthy life for your French Bulldog.

Always remember that each French Bulldog is unique and may require specific care. Observe your pet, learn about their individual needs and adapt care accordingly. Don't hesitate to consult your veterinarian for personalized advice and to provide your French Bulldog with the best possible care.

I hope this second part of the chapter on basic French Bulldog care has been useful to you and will help you keep your pet happy and healthy!

Chapter 7: Common French Bulldog Health and Diseases

It explores the possible diseases and health conditions that French Bulldogs are prone to, as well as ways to prevent and treat them.

The French Bulldog is a breed known for its beauty and charming personality. However, just like any living being, these adorable dogs can be affected by various diseases and health conditions. It's important for pet owners to be aware of them to provide proper care and ensure a long and healthy life for their French Bulldogs.

One of the most common health conditions in French Bulldogs is respiratory distress. Because of their flat facial structure, these dogs may have trouble breathing properly. This is due to a condition known as Brachycephalic Syndrome or Brachycephaly, which affects breeds with short, flat skulls. To prevent complications, it's critical to avoid strenuous exercise on hot days and to ensure that they always have access to fresh water.

In addition to respiratory problems, French Bulldogs are also prone to dermatological problems. Your soft, delicate skin may be prone to infections, allergies, and skin rashes. It's important to maintain good hygiene, regularly cleaning your skin folds and avoiding irritating chemicals. If redness, itching or bad smell is observed on the French Bulldog's skin, it is advisable to go to the vet for proper diagnosis and treatment.

Obesity is another common problem in this breed. French Bulldogs have a voracious appetite and tend to gain weight quickly if their diet is not controlled. Being overweight can worsen breathing problems and increase the risk of heart disease and orthopedic disorders. Owners should provide a balanced diet and control their pet's food portions, as well as ensure they provide enough exercise to keep them in shape.

Intervertebral disc disease is another condition that can affect French Bulldogs. This disease affects the discs between the vertebrae of the spine and can cause pain, weakness, and even paralysis. Proper weight management and avoiding excessive jumps can help prevent this disease. If signs of pain or difficulty moving are observed, it is essential to go to the vet quickly.

Last but not least, French Bulldogs are prone to eye problems. They can develop diseases such as cataracts, glaucoma, corneal ulcers, and entropion. Proper eye care, such as regular cleaning and attention to any signs of redness, excessive secretion, or change in appearance, can help prevent eye complications.

In short, French Bulldogs are an adorable breed that is prone to various diseases and health conditions. However, most of these problems can be prevented or treated properly with proper care and regular visits to the vet. By knowing the peculiarities of this breed and being attentive to the signs of their pet, owners can guarantee a happy and healthy life for their French Bulldog.

The second half of this chapter will focus on other common diseases affecting French Bulldogs, as well as additional preventive measures and treatment options.

One of the diseases that French Bulldog owners should be aware of his hip dysplasia. This condition is characterized by abnormal development of the hip joint and can lead to mobility problems, pain and lameness. To prevent or control hip dysplasia, it is advisable to keep French Bulldogs at a healthy weight and avoid activities that are too demanding on their joints, such as jumping or running on hard surfaces. In addition, some vets may recommend supplements that promote joint health.

Another common disorder in French Bulldogs is gastric dilatation-volvulus, also known as gastric torsion. This condition occurs when a dog's stomach swells and twists, which can be life threatening if not treated quickly. Symptoms of gastric torsion include abdominal bloating, restlessness, repeated vomiting, and an inability to defecate. If gastric torsion is suspected, it is important to seek emergency veterinary care immediately. To prevent this condition, it is recommended to feed French Bulldogs small, frequent meals, rather than one large meal a day, and to avoid strenuous exercise immediately after eating.

Brachycephalic dog syndrome is another problem affecting French Bulldogs because of their flat facial structure. This syndrome refers to the chronic respiratory problems that these dogs face, such as hypopnea and loud snoring. Although there is no cure for this syndrome, steps can be taken to improve the quality of life of affected French Bulldogs. This includes keeping dogs in a cool, well-ventilated environment, avoiding extreme heat, and providing them with raised beds to help facilitate breathing while they sleep.

In addition, French Bulldogs can be prone to heart problems, such as aortic stenosis and degenerative valve disease. These conditions can affect the heart's ability to pump blood effectively and can cause symptoms such as fatigue, weakness, and shortness of breath. If a heart problem is suspected, it is essential to go to the vet for an accurate diagnosis and an appropriate treatment plan.

It's essential that French Bulldog owners be aware of any changes in their pet's behavior, appetite, weight, or activity. Any signs of illness should be taken seriously and consulted with a trusted veterinarian. In addition, maintaining good hygiene, providing a balanced diet and controlling your dog's weight are key preventive measures to ensure a long and healthy life for your French Bulldog.

In conclusion, French Bulldogs can be prone to various diseases and health conditions. However, with proper care and care, most of these diseases can be successfully prevented or treated. French Bulldog owners must be aware of the peculiarities and medical needs of this charming breed to provide them with the best possible care and ensure their long-term well-being. Your love and understanding will be critical to maintaining your French Bulldog's health and happiness.

Chapter 8: Sterilization and reproduction of the French Bulldog

Evaluate the convenience of sterilizing your French Bulldog and learn what are the processes and precautions to consider if you choose to seek their reproduction.

Spaying and breeding are two important aspects to consider when you have a French Bulldog as a pet. Both sterilization and reproduction are decisions that must be taken with care, taking into account the well-being of the dog and considering the individual circumstances of each owner.

Sterilization, also known as castration in the case of males and as ovariohysterectomy in females, involves the surgical removal of the dog's reproductive organs. This practice has benefits for both the dog's health and its behavior.

In the case of French Bulldogs, sterilization may be especially recommended due to some particular breed conditions. Being a brachycephalic breed, that is, with a flat facial structure, these dogs can have respiratory difficulties and problems associated with heat. Spaying can help reduce agitation and stress in the dog, which could decrease the respiratory and temperature problems they face.

In addition to the health benefits, sterilization also prevents indiscriminate breeding and contributes to the control of the dog population. French Bulldogs are a popular breed, and unfortunately, many of them end up in shelters or in the hands of unscrupulous breeders. Sterilization helps prevent unwanted reproduction and the proliferation of puppies that could not be properly cared for or that could end up abandoned.

However, the decision to sterilize your French Bulldog must be evaluated on an individual basis. If you intend to raise your dog and have the knowledge, resources and time necessary to carry out responsible breeding, then you can consider not sterilizing it. But it is important to mention that dog reproduction entails responsibilities and requirements that not all owners can assume.

If you decide to seek the reproduction of your French Bulldog, it is essential to follow a meticulous process to ensure the well-being of the mother and the puppies. Before starting breeding, it is essential to check the health of both dogs and rule out any diseases or genetic abnormalities. In addition, it is important to look for a male of optimal quality and health to ensure the quality of the litter.

During the breeding process, close monitoring of the female is essential. Adequate veterinary monitoring and adequate nutrition are essential to ensure a healthy pregnancy and the proper development of puppies. It's also important to be prepared for any complications that may arise during delivery and to have the support of an experienced veterinarian.

In conclusion, French Bulldog sterilization and breeding are important decisions that must be carefully evaluated. Sterilization can provide health benefits for dogs and contribute to population control, while breeding requires careful attention and additional responsibilities. Whatever decision you make, always remember to ensure the well-being of your French Bulldog and the canine community in general.

During the breeding process of the French Bulldog, it is essential to take into account a series of additional precautions and care to ensure the health and well-being of the mother and the puppies.

Before starting breeding, it is essential to carry out a thorough veterinary examination of both the female and the male. This includes genetic testing to rule out inherited diseases that could be transmitted to the litter. In addition, it is important to ensure that both dogs are in optimal health and have all their vaccines and deworming up to date.

Once the dogs' health has been confirmed and a quality male has been chosen, it is important to be prepared for the time of mating. The female must be in her estrus period, which usually occurs around day 11 to 14 of the cycle, and will show signs of receptivity such as lifting her tail or allowing her to be ridden by the male.

During the mating act, it's crucial to closely monitor the dogs to ensure that everything goes safely and without complications. An experienced veterinarian can provide advice and be present to help if any problems or difficulties arise.

Once the female has been successfully covered, it is important to monitor her gestation status. During this period, you must provide him with an adequate and balanced diet, rich in nutrients necessary for the development of puppies. Also, be sure to keep her away from stressful situations and to do intense physical exercises that could endanger her health or that of the puppies.

As your pregnancy progresses, you must prepare an area suitable for delivery. A quiet and clean place, with a comfortable bed for the mother and the puppies, will be essential to ensure their safety and well-being. In addition, you must have all the items necessary to attend the delivery, such as clean towels, umbilical clamps and sterilized scissors, on hand.

Once it's time for delivery, it's important to be prepared for any complications that may arise. While most of the time the delivery goes smoothly, there are cases in which it may be necessary to intervene to help the mother or the puppies. In these cases, having the support of an experienced veterinarian is essential.

After puppies are born, it is essential to provide them with the necessary care for their proper development. This includes making sure they are nourished properly, offering them breast milk or an appropriate replacement if the mother is unable to breastfeed. It's also important to ensure that they are kept in a warm environment free of any factors that could pose a risk to their health.

In short, the reproduction of the French Bulldog requires additional care and precautions to ensure the well-being of the mother and the puppies. From previous veterinary exams, to the time of mating and follow-up during pregnancy and delivery, it's crucial to be attentive and supported by experienced professionals. Always remember to put the welfare of dogs first and to take on the additional responsibilities that come with breeding this wonderful breed.

Chapter 9: The French Bulldog and the Children

Learn how the French Bulldog can be an excellent companion and protector for children, as long as certain interaction guidelines are met.

The French Bulldog is a dog breed known for its charming personality and its ability to adapt to diverse environments. They are loyal and loving companions, making them an ideal option to share with the youngest members of the family. However, it is essential to understand the appropriate dynamics and patterns of interaction to ensure the safety and well-being of both children and the French Bulldog.

One of the main characteristics of the French Bulldog is its patience and kindness towards children. They are patient dogs by nature and enjoy the company of the little ones. In addition, their compact size and quiet nature make them a suitable breed for living in homes with limited space.

When it comes to integrating a French Bulldog into a family environment with children, it is essential to teach them from the beginning how to properly interact with the dog. Children must learn to respect the dog's space and never disturb him while he sleeps or eats. It is also essential to teach them to caress the dog in a gentle and delicate way, avoiding sudden movements that could scare it.

In addition, it is recommended to always monitor interactions between children and the French Bulldog, especially when they are very young. Although French Bulldogs are usually friendly and tolerant, you can never fully predict a dog's reaction, so it's important to be attentive and willing to intervene if necessary.

It's crucial to remember that, as pet owners, our primary responsibility is to ensure that both the children and the dog are safe and comfortable. We should never leave a child alone with a dog, regardless of the breed. Constant monitoring is essential to avoid any type of accident or uncomfortable situation.

Although the French Bulldog can be an excellent companion for children, it's important to note that every dog is unique and has its own personality. Some may be more tolerant and playful, while others may prefer moments of tranquility and rest. It is essential to respect the individual preferences and needs of each dog to ensure a harmonious coexistence.

In short, the French Bulldog can be a wonderful companion and protector for children, as long as certain guidelines for interaction and supervision are followed. Patience, mutual respect and constant vigilance are essential to ensure a positive relationship between children and their furry friend. With proper care and attention, the French Bulldog can play an important role in children's lives, providing them with companionship and unconditional love.

As children grow, it is important to actively involve them in the care and education of the French Bulldog. This will not only teach them responsibility, but it will also strengthen the bond between the child and their pet.

One way to encourage this participation is to assign tasks appropriate to the child's age. For example, younger children can help feed the dog under adult supervision, while older children can take care of walking the dog or brushing it. This will not only help the French Bulldog stay healthy and happy, but it will also teach children about animal care and teamwork.

In addition, it is important to teach children to read the behavioral cues of the French Bulldog. This will help them to better understand your dog's emotions and needs, and to respond appropriately. For example, if the French Bulldog is agitated or uncomfortable, it's essential that children step away and give him space. This will teach them to respect the dog's limits and to avoid stressful situations for both of them.

It is also essential to remember that children must learn to be consistent in their treatment with the French Bulldog. Establishing clear and consistent boundaries from the start will help avoid confusion and ensure that the dog understands the rules of living together. This includes teaching children not to pull on the dog's fur or ears, or to treat the dog abruptly or aggressively.

As the relationship between the French Bulldog and children strengthens, it's important to take advantage of opportunities for them to play and have fun together. Interactive games, such as throwing a soft ball for the dog to catch, can be a great way to keep both of you active and stimulated. You can also promote the bond between the child and the dog through activities such as reading stories to the French Bulldog, which will provide them with moments of calm and connection.

If there are behavioral problems or difficulties in the interaction between the French Bulldog and children, it is advisable to seek the help of a canine behavior professional. These experts will be able to provide personalized guidance and advice to address any specific situation.

In conclusion, the French Bulldog can be an excellent companion for children, as long as adequate interaction guidelines are established and constant supervision is provided. Patience, mutual respect and education are essential to maintaining a harmonious relationship between children and their beloved dog. By following these recommendations, pet owners can enjoy the benefits of having a French Bulldog in the family, providing children with loyal companionship and unconditional love.

Chapter 10: Living with other animals

Learn how to introduce your French Bulldog to an environment where other animals live together and how to promote harmonious relationships between them.

Living with other animals can be a challenge for any pet owner, especially when it comes to introducing a French Bulldog to that scenario. Although these charming canines are known for their sociable and friendly personalities, each French Bulldog has their own way of interacting with other animals. In this chapter, we'll explore the key steps for introducing your French Bulldog to other animals and how to foster harmonious relationships between them.

Before taking your French Bulldog to an environment where other animals live together, it is essential to consider the needs and temperament of your pet. Like humans, dogs can have individual preferences when interacting with other animals and it's important to respect them. Some French Bulldogs may be more tolerant of other dogs, while others may be more cautious or even dominant. Observe your French Bulldog's behavior and reactions to determine how he feels about other animals.

A gradual and controlled introduction is the key to creating a positive experience for your French Bulldog and the other animals. It starts with short meetings in a neutral environment, such as a park or an open area. Keep your French Bulldog on a leash and praise his good behavior during these first few encounters. If you notice signs of stress or discomfort in your French Bulldog, take a step back and make sure he feels safe and calm before continuing.

During the introduction process, it's essential to closely monitor the interaction between your French Bulldog and the other animals. Watch their body language and be sure to intervene if there are any signs of aggression or tension. If your French Bulldog shows dominant behaviors, such as being dominant or trying to establish its hierarchy, seek the help of a professional trainer to address these issues appropriately.

In addition to the introduction, there are several techniques to promote harmonious relationships between your French Bulldog and other animals. Positive reinforcement is a powerful tool when training your pet to behave appropriately. Reward your French Bulldog when they interact in a friendly way with other animals, whether through petting, praise or small treats. This will strengthen your positive association with the company of other animals.

Patience and consistency are essential during this socialization process. Each French Bulldog has its own rhythm and it can take time to adapt to living with other animals. Don't be discouraged if the results don't come right away, continue working on training and providing support to your French Bulldog.

In short, living with other animals can be a rewarding experience for both your French Bulldog and you. Remember to consider your pet's individual needs, make gradual, controlled introductions, and use positive reinforcement techniques. Patience and commitment are essential to achieving harmonious relationships between your French Bulldog and other animals. In the second half of this chapter, we'll explore some additional strategies for consolidating these relationships and addressing potential challenges. Keep reading to find out more! Once you've done the initial introductions and your French Bulldog feels comfortable around other animals, it's important to continue to foster harmonious relationships. In this second half of the chapter, we'll explore some additional strategies for consolidating these relationships and addressing potential challenges.

One of the most effective ways to promote peaceful relationships between your French Bulldog and other animals is through supervised play. Organizing play sessions with dogs or animals of other species can help strengthen the bonds between them and encourage a playful and friendly attitude. During these sessions, be sure to watch the interactions closely and be ready to intervene if necessary. If you see signs of aggression or tension, stop playing and redirect their attention to calmer, more enjoyable activities.

In addition to supervised play, it's useful to teach your French Bulldog basic obedience commands. This will not only provide them with a solid foundation for training, but it will also help them to maintain friendly and calm behavior in the presence of other animals. Teach them commands such as "sitting", "still" and "come here", and positively reinforce their good behavior every time they follow them correctly.

Continuous socialization is another key aspect to promote harmonious coexistence with other animals. Exposing your French Bulldog to different situations, environments and animals from an early age will help them adapt and feel comfortable in a variety of circumstances. Taking your French Bulldog to dog parks, play dates and group walks can be beneficial for their socialization and will allow them to interact with other animals in a controlled environment.

It's important to note that every French Bulldog is unique and may have different levels of tolerance towards other animals. Some may enjoy the company of dogs and cats, while others may feel more comfortable in the presence of smaller animals such as rabbits or birds. Always watch your French Bulldog and respect their individual preferences when choosing the environment in which they interact with other animals.

However, you may face challenges during your French Bulldog's socialization process with other animals. If you're experiencing difficulties, consider seeking help from an animal behavior professional or dog trainer. They'll be able to assess the situation, identify problem areas, and provide you with additional strategies to address any conflict or unwanted behavior.

In conclusion, harmonious coexistence with other animals is possible for your French Bulldog. Through supervised play, teaching basic obedience commands and continuous socialization, you can strengthen your French Bulldog's relationships with other animals and promote a peaceful and happy environment. Always remember to respect your pet's individual preferences and watch for any signs of tension or aggression. Patience and empathy will be your best allies in this adventure of living with other animals.

Chapter 11: The French Bulldog in apartments and small spaces

Discover how the French Bulldog adapts perfectly to living in apartments and small spaces, as long as their needs for activity and stimulation are met.

French Bulldogs are known for their charming personality and their ability to adapt to different environments, including living in apartments and small spaces. Although they are small dogs, don't be fooled by their size, as they have great energy and character. However, despite their charming personality, it's critical to understand their needs to ensure that we provide them with a suitable environment.

Space is no problem for a French Bulldog as long as their needs for activity and stimulation are met. While they don't need huge backyards or large parks to run, they do need daily exercise and opportunities to expend their energy. For this reason, it's essential that owners of French Bulldogs in apartments or small spaces commit to providing them with adequate exercise and stimulation.

One of the most effective ways to keep a French Bulldog happy and healthy in an apartment is to take him out for regular walks. Although they don't need long or strenuous walks, they enjoy daily walks that allow them to explore their environment. These walks not only provide them with physical exercise, but also mental stimulation by being exposed to different smells, sounds and sights.

Another option to meet the exercise needs of a French Bulldog in a small space is indoor play. These dogs really enjoy interactive games with their owners, such as throwing balls at them that they can chase or search toys that keep them entertained. In addition, there are interactive toys designed specifically for dogs that provide them with mental and physical stimulation, such as puzzles or prize dispensing toys.

It's important to remember that the French Bulldog is a brachycephalic breed, meaning that its cranial structure can make it difficult to breathe in hot weather or during strenuous activities. For this reason, it's essential to avoid excessive exercise on hot days and to provide them with a cool, shaded environment when they're indoors.

In addition to physical exercise, French Bulldogs need mental stimulation to avoid potential destructive behavior or boredom. There are several ways to provide them with this stimulation, such as offering them chewing toys, teaching them new tricks or commands, or even practicing obedience training.

When living in apartments or small spaces, it's important to note that French Bulldogs can be sensitive to loud noises or excessive stimuli. Therefore, it is advisable to create a calm and safe environment for them, avoiding excessive exposure to noise or stressful situations.

In short, the French Bulldog is perfectly suited to living in apartments and small spaces as long as their needs for activity and stimulation are met. Regular walks, interactive indoor play, and mental stimulation are critical to keeping these dogs happy and balanced. Also remember to provide them with a cool and safe environment, avoiding excessive exposure to noise or stressful situations. In the second part of this chapter, we'll explore other important aspects to consider to ensure the well-being and comfort of your French Bulldog in a cramped environment. Keep reading for more helpful tips! Once we have established an appropriate exercise and stimulation routine for our French Bulldog in an apartment or small space, we must also ensure that they are comfortable in their environment.

First of all, it is essential to provide them with a suitable place to rest. French Bulldogs love having their own quiet, cozy space where they can relax and unwind. We can place a comfortable, fluffy bed in a corner of the apartment, away from noise and distractions, so they can retire when they need to.

In addition, we must pay attention to the temperature of the environment. As we mentioned earlier, French Bulldogs are brachycephalic dogs and can have difficulty breathing in hot weather. Therefore, it is important to keep the apartment cool and provide them with access to fresh water at all times. In addition, we can use fans or air conditioning to maintain the right temperature in the space.

Another aspect to consider is the safety of the environment. French Bulldogs can be curious and explorers, so it's important to secure all objects and furniture that may pose a danger to them. This includes properly securing windows and balconies, keeping chemicals or toxic plants out of reach, and placing protectors on sharp corners or electrical cables.

In addition, it is essential to consider the socialization of the French Bulldog. Although they are friendly and sociable dogs by nature, it is important that they have interaction with other dogs and people to maintain their emotional balance and avoid potential behavioral problems. We can organize play dates with other dogs or take them to dog parks where they can socialize safely.

Food also plays an important role in the well-being of our French Bulldog. We must ensure that we provide them with a balanced diet appropriate to their age and needs. Consulting with a veterinarian will help us establish the best feeding plan for our dog.

Finally, we cannot forget the importance of providing them with affection and care on a daily basis. French Bulldogs are very loyal and affectionate dogs, and they need to feel loved and valued by their owners. Spending quality time with them, caressing them and playing together will strengthen our bond with them and provide them with a sense of security and happiness.

In conclusion, the French Bulldog is excellently suited to living in apartments and small spaces as long as their needs for activity, stimulation and comfort are met. Providing them with daily exercise, mental stimulation, a fresh and safe environment, and adequate nutrition are key to their well-being. In addition, we must pay attention to their rest, socialization and affection. With the right care, our French Bulldog will be able to enjoy a happy and healthy life in a small space. Always remember to check with a vet for personalized guidance and to make sure your dog is in the best possible condition!

Chapter 12: French Bulldog and physical exercise

Explore the importance of physical exercise for the French Bulldog and discover different activities you can do with him to keep him healthy and fit.

The French Bulldog is a breed of dog that is characterized by its charming personality and its peculiar appearance. Although its appearance can deceive us and lead us to think that it is a lazy or inactive dog, this couldn't be further from the truth. Despite its compact size, the French Bulldog needs regular physical exercise to stay happy and healthy.

Exercise is essential for any dog, as it helps them maintain a healthy weight, strengthen their muscles and release accumulated energy. In the case of the French Bulldog, this is especially important, as their tendency to suffer respiratory problems can worsen if they are not kept in an optimal physical state. In addition, exercise also helps to stimulate your mind and improve your behavior.

Although the French Bulldog doesn't require the same amount of exercise as other, more energetic breeds, it's essential to ensure that they receive physical activity appropriate to their needs. One of the most recommended activities for this breed is daily walking. Use this time to mentally stimulate him and socialize him with other dogs and people. However, be aware of extreme weather conditions and temperatures, as the French Bulldog is sensitive to heat and can suffer from heat stroke.

In addition to the walk, there are other fun and beneficial options for exercising your French Bulldog. One of them is the interactive game, both indoors and outdoors. You can use interactive toys or search games to stimulate his hunting instinct and keep him entertained. You can also teach him simple tricks, such as sitting or pawing, through short, fun training sessions.

Another activity that French Bulldogs enjoy a lot is swimming. Although not all dogs have the same affinity for water, many French Bulldogs are excellent swimmers and have a great time in the water. However, before taking him swimming, make sure he knows how to get out of the pool or the place where you are going to practice this activity, to avoid accidents.

Remember that the French Bulldog may have difficulty breathing due to its flat facial structure. For this reason, it is essential to exercise caution when performing intense exercise or in environments with high temperatures. Watch your dog closely during physical activity and stop if you notice that he is getting exhausted or has trouble breathing. Not all French Bulldogs are the same, so it's important to adapt the exercise to your individual physical condition.

In short, physical exercise is vital to keeping your French Bulldog fit and happy. Although they don't need the same amount of exercise as some more active breeds, it's essential to provide them with activities that stimulate both their body and mind. Daily walking, interactive play, swimming and training are great options to keep your French Bulldog healthy and energetic. However, always remember to consider the limitations of this breed and adapt the exercise to your individual needs.

The French Bulldog is a breed of dog with a charming personality and physical peculiarities that make them special. In the first half of this chapter, we explored the importance of physical exercise in keeping French Bulldogs happy and healthy. Now, we'll continue to discover more activities and practical tips to provide these adorable companions with the right exercise routines.

Another activity that can be beneficial for the French Bulldog is agility. Agility consists of performing a series of obstacles on a specific circuit, such as jumps, tunnels and walkways. Although it may seem like a more suitable activity for energetic and athletic dogs, French Bulldogs can also participate and enjoy it. It is always important to adapt the level of difficulty and intensity to the dog's physical condition. Even if your French Bulldog isn't competing professionally, agility can be a fun way to keep him active and stimulate his mind.

In addition to agility, another interesting option is the use of treadmills for dogs. These straps allow your French Bulldog to exercise indoors, especially when the weather conditions aren't ideal for going out. It is important to ensure that the dog is comfortable and safe while exercising on the treadmill, so it is advisable to monitor him and adjust the speed and duration of training according to his individual needs.

Smell training is also a great way to exercise your French Bulldog. These dogs have an excellent sense of smell and enjoy looking for and finding objects. You can hide treats or toys around the house or garden and stimulate their search instinct. This type of game will not only provide physical exercise, but it will also provide mental stimulation that will be very beneficial in keeping your French Bulldog healthy and happy.

In addition, keep in mind that a balanced diet adapted to the needs of your French Bulldog is also essential for their overall well-being. Check with your vet to make sure you are providing him with the right diet and adjust the amount of food according to his level of physical activity.

Always remember to watch your dog during physical activity and stop if you notice signs of exhaustion or difficulty breathing. Each French Bulldog is unique and may have different levels of exercise tolerance. Pay attention to your dog's limits and adapt activities and intensity to their individual needs.

In conclusion, physical exercise is essential to keep your French Bulldog healthy and happy. From daily walking to interactive play, swimming and agility, there are many fun and beneficial options for exercising this fantastic breed. Always remember to adapt the exercise to your dog's specific needs and provide him with a balanced diet. With the right care, your French Bulldog will enjoy an active and energetic life with you. So don't hesitate to start enjoying all these activities with your canine companion!

Chapter 13: Traveling with your French Bulldog

Learn how to plan trips and trips with your French Bulldog, considering their safety, comfort and special needs along the way.

Traveling with your French Bulldog can become a wonderful and memorable experience, both for you and for your loyal companion. However, it's important to note that these adorable dogs have certain peculiarities and needs that must be taken care of while traveling. In this chapter, we'll provide you with valuable tips for planning your trips with your faithful French Bulldog.

Your pet's safety should always be your number one priority when traveling. Make sure you have an appropriate restraint system, such as a harness or seat belt specially designed for dogs. This will prevent your French Bulldog from moving dangerously inside the vehicle and reduce the risk of accidents. Never leave your pet loose in the car, as this can be extremely dangerous for both him and the passengers.

In addition, it's essential that you plan your stops during the trip. French Bulldogs are prone to respiratory problems, especially in warm climates. Therefore, it is advisable to make frequent stops to allow them to rest, hydrate and cool down. Look for shaded areas where you can park your vehicle and allow your pet to stretch its legs and relax.

During the journey, be sure to carry fresh water and a special container so that your French Bulldog can drink comfortably. Remember that these puppies are prone to dehydration, so it's essential to keep them hydrated at all times. In addition, avoid overfeeding them before starting the trip, as this could cause an upset stomach or nausea during the journey.

Another important aspect to consider is the comfort of your French Bulldog during the trip. If you are traveling by car, be sure to prepare the area where your pet will be located. Use a soft mat or pillow so you can rest comfortably. Also, avoid exposing him to direct drafts or extreme temperatures, which could affect his health and well-being.

Similarly, if you're planning to travel by plane or other mode of transportation, research the airline's or transportation company's policies and requirements ahead of time. Some companies require dogs to travel in specific containers and to meet certain documentation requirements. Make sure you're informed and prepared to comply with all regulations.

In short, traveling with a French Bulldog requires special planning to ensure the safety, comfort and well-being of your pet. Remember to ensure their proper support, make frequent stops for rest and hydration, and keep them comfortable during the ride. In the second half of this chapter, we'll provide you with more practical tips so you can enjoy your travels with your charming French Bulldog. Don't miss it!

To be continued... The second half of this chapter will focus on providing you with more practical advice so that you can fully enjoy your trips with your charming French Bulldog. Let's continue to explore ways to care for your pet while traveling.

If you're planning a long trip by car, it's important to bring a first aid kit for your French Bulldog with you. This will allow you to be prepared in case of any eventuality. Your first aid kit should include basic items such as gauze, bandages, alcohol and hydrogen peroxide. Also, make sure you have emergency veterinary telephone numbers handy in each of the areas you are going to travel through. This way, you can act quickly if complications arise during the trip.

Remember that French Bulldogs are sensitive to temperature changes and extreme climates. If you're traveling to a place with very low temperatures, such as in winter, consider taking a suitable coat or sweater with you to keep your pet warm. In the same way, if you go to a place with very high temperatures, make sure you have an efficient air conditioning system in the vehicle, to ensure that your French Bulldog does not suffer from heat stroke.

Another important recommendation is to take some toys or distracting items with you to entertain your pet during the trip. French Bulldogs are intelligent and active animals, so they need to stay stimulated and entertained while on the go. Rubber or plush toys are ideal for keeping your dog busy and reducing his anxiety.

If you are planning to travel by plane with your French Bulldog, it is essential that you inform yourself in advance about the policies and requirements of the airline you will be flying with. Some companies require dogs to travel on specific carriers, meeting certain size and ventilation requirements. In addition, up-to-date health and vaccination certificates may be requested. Make sure you comply with all regulations to avoid setbacks and ensure a safe and stress-free trip for your pet.

It's always helpful to research and seek recommendations for destinations that are dog-friendly. Not all cities or establishments accept pets, so planning ahead will be key to avoiding inconvenience. Nowadays, many hotels, restaurants and tourist places have adapted and allow dogs to enter, even offering special services for them. Look for accommodation options and establishments that are pet-friendly, so you can make the most of your trip with your French Bulldog.

In conclusion, traveling with your French Bulldog can be a wonderful experience if you plan properly and take care of their safety, comfort and special needs. Remember to bring a first aid kit, be prepared for temperature changes, and entertain your pet during the trip. Research air travel policies and look for destinations that are dog-friendly. By following these tips, you can create unforgettable memories with your faithful companion. Happy travels!

Chapter 14: French Bulldog and its relationship to the climate

Learn how the French Bulldog can adapt to different climates and how to protect it from extreme temperatures to preserve its health and well-being.

In this chapter, we'll explore the fascinating ability of the French Bulldog to adapt to diverse climates. Although these adorable canines are native to France, their ability to acclimate to different temperatures is truly amazing.

The French Bulldog has a characteristic and peculiar appearance, with its muscular and compact body, so distinctive of the breed. However, despite their robust appearance, these dogs do not tolerate extreme climates well, whether cold or hot. That's why it's crucial that the owners of these charming canine companions take the necessary precautions to protect them from the harshest weather conditions.

When it comes to cold climates, it's important to remember that the French Bulldog is not very cold resistant. Because of their body structure and short coat, they are more prone to feeling the cold intensely. Therefore, during the winter or in cold climates, it is essential to provide them with adequate shelter and to limit exposure to extreme cold.

An excellent option to protect your French Bulldog from the cold is to provide clothing designed especially for dogs. A wide variety of sweaters, jackets and coats are available on the market. Not only will these garments provide warmth, but they will also make them look even more adorable.

In addition to warm clothing, it is essential to provide them with a warm and comfortable bed in an area of the house that is well insulated. Avoid placing their bed near drafts and make sure they stay away from cold areas, such as tile floors or concrete. Also, consider using thermal blankets for dogs, which will allow them to maintain an adequate body temperature.

In contrast, when faced with hot climates, the French Bulldog can struggle to regulate its body temperature due to its inherent inability to breathe properly. These dogs have a flat nose and a narrower trachea, making it difficult for them to dissipate body heat. Therefore, it is essential to take steps to keep them cool and protect them from excessive heat.

During hot days, avoid taking your French Bulldog out for a walk during the hottest hours of the day. Choose to go for walks early in the morning or in the late afternoon, when the temperatures are milder. In addition, it's crucial to provide them with constant access to fresh water, and to consider using a cooling vest for dogs, which will help regulate their body temperature.

It is important to mention that the French Bulldog is more prone to heat stroke compared to other breeds. Symptoms of heat stroke in a dog can include excessive panting, difficulty breathing, weakness, lethargy, and in severe cases, even loss of consciousness. If you suspect that your French Bulldog is experiencing heat stroke, you should act quickly and seek veterinary care immediately.

In conclusion, the French Bulldog is a dog with a charming personality that can adapt to different climates, as long as it is given the right care. In both cold and hot climates, it's essential to provide them with shelter, appropriate clothing, and to keep an eye out for signs of discomfort due to extreme weather conditions. Remember, your French Bulldog's well-being depends on you, and together they can face any weather! It is essential to be aware that the French Bulldog cannot withstand extreme temperatures, whether cold or hot. In the second half of this chapter, we'll dive deeper into how to protect these adorable canine companions from hot climates and how to ensure their well-being during these adverse conditions.

When faced with hot climates, French Bulldogs can be especially vulnerable because of their inherent difficulty in regulating their body temperature. One of the most important things you can do is to make sure they always have access to fresh water. Place several water containers in accessible areas of the house and regularly check that they are full. This way, they can properly hydrate and refresh themselves when they need it.

In addition, it is advisable to provide them with a cool, well-ventilated place where they can rest during hot days. Avoid leaving them in the sun and make sure they have enough shade in the yard or garden. If possible, consider using an air conditioning system or fans to keep the internal temperature of the house comfortable for your French Bulldog. This will help them stay cool and comfortable even on the hottest days.

Another option you can consider is the use of cooling vests for dogs. These vests are designed to keep your French Bulldog's body temperature regulated during warm climates. They work by absorbing water and evaporating, providing a cooling effect on the dog. Cooling vests are a great way to protect your pet from the negative effects of excessive heat.

As we mentioned earlier, the French Bulldog is more prone to heat stroke compared to other breeds. Heatstroke can be extremely dangerous and potentially fatal. Therefore, it's essential that you watch for signs of discomfort or heat stress in your French Bulldog. If you notice that you're panting excessively, having trouble breathing, feeling weak or lethargic, it's important to act quickly.

If you suspect that your French Bulldog is suffering from heat stroke, it's crucial to get him to a cool place right away and provide him with fresh water to drink. Moisturizing your body with room temperature or slightly cool water can also be beneficial. However, it is important to remember that ice water should not be used, as this can cause thermal shock. It's also critical to seek immediate veterinary care, as heat strokes can be life threatening and require professional treatment.

In short, French Bulldogs are charming dogs that can adapt to different climates when given the right care. During hot climates, remember to provide them with constant access to fresh water, ensure they have a cool, shady place to rest, consider using cooling vests, and watch for signs of heat stroke. By taking these precautions, you'll be ensuring the well-being and health of your French Bulldog, even in the most challenging weather conditions.

Always remember to be aware of the specific needs of your French Bulldog and to adapt these recommendations to their individual situation. Your love and dedication are essential to ensure that your French Bulldog feels comfortable and protected in any weather. Together they can face the challenges of the climate and enjoy a relationship full of love and happiness.

Chapter 15: The Importance of Veterinary Check-Ups

The well-being of our beloved French Bulldogs is a responsibility that we should not take lightly. By caring for these wonderful creatures, we become their protectors and are responsible for providing them with a healthy and happy life. One of the keys to ensuring this is regular veterinary checkups, which play a fundamental role in their health and longevity.

The French Bulldog is a breed that is as fascinating as it is delicate. Their unique facial structure and compact body make them dogs prone to certain health conditions. For this reason, veterinary checkups are essential to detect any problems early and provide them with appropriate treatment.

During these checkups, the vet thoroughly examines our inseparable companion. Do a general physical evaluation, paying special attention to your heart, lungs, and digestive system. Also check their eyes and ears, as French Bulldogs can often suffer from eye problems or ear infections.

In addition, the vet will regularly measure the blood pressure of our little furry friend. It is surprising that these adorable dogs can have problems with hypertension, which can lead to serious cardiovascular diseases if not treated in time. Through these checkups, we can detect any changes in your blood pressure and take preventive measures.

Blood testing is another essential part of veterinary checkups. Through it, we can learn in detail about the health of our French Bulldog, evaluate their kidney and liver function, and detect possible nutritional deficiencies. A urine test is also done to assess your kidney health and rule out any underlying infection or disease.

We cannot forget the importance of radiographic examinations in veterinary checkups. These x-rays allow us to visualize the state of the bones and joints of our French Bulldog, a particular concern in this breed. Bulldogs are prone to hip dysplasia, a painful condition that can limit their mobility. Detecting it early gives us the opportunity to seek the best treatment to ease your pain and improve your quality of life.

In addition to all these evaluations, the veterinarian will also be attentive to possible warning signs that we must consider as responsible owners. Sudden weight gain or loss, changes in appetite, abnormal behavior, frequent vomiting, or persistent diarrhea may be symptoms of an underlying condition that requires immediate attention. Being alert to these signs and communicating any changes to the vet is crucial to the care of our French Bulldog.

In conclusion, regular veterinary checkups are a fundamental part of caring for our beloved French Bulldogs. These regular visits make it possible to detect and treat health problems early, ensuring a long and happy life for our furry companions. So don't forget to schedule the next appointment with your vet, your Bulldog will thank you! During regular veterinary checkups, not only is the physical condition of our French Bulldog assessed, but emotional and behavioral aspects are also addressed to ensure their overall well-being. It's important to remember that these adorable furry animals are extremely loyal and affectionate animals, and their emotional needs should not be overlooked.

During the visit to the vet, attention will be paid to any changes in the behavior of the French Bulldog. Sometimes, they may show signs of anxiety or stress, which can be caused by a variety of factors such as changes in their environment, socialization problems, or even physical pain. The veterinarian will know how to identify warning signs and provide recommendations to help alleviate any emotional distress that our faithful companion may be experiencing.

In addition, the veterinarian can offer guidance and advice on proper nutrition for the French Bulldog. This breed tends to have problems with being overweight, so a balanced and controlled diet is essential to keep their weight healthy and prevent associated diseases, such as diabetes or heart problems. A well-fed French Bulldog is a happy and vibrant dog.

Another important aspect to consider during veterinary checkups is the prevention of parasites. These small intruders can affect the health of our French Bulldogs and cause various diseases. Your veterinarian can recommend the best products and methods to prevent both internal and external flea, tick, and worm infestations. Keeping our Bulldog protected against these parasites is essential for their long-term well-being.

In the case of females, it is also essential to discuss reproductive planning during veterinary checkups. Responsible breeding of French Bulldogs is of the utmost importance to maintain the health of the breed and avoid hereditary genetic problems. The veterinarian can provide advice on the right time for sterilization or castration, as well as on best practices in controlled reproduction.

Last but not least, veterinary checkups also provide an opportunity for pet owners to voice any concerns or questions related to the health of their French Bulldog. No question is too insignificant when it comes to the well-being of our furry companion. The vet is there to answer all our questions and provide the necessary information to ensure a happy and healthy life for our beloved French Bulldog.

In conclusion, veterinary checkups not only focus on the physical health of our French Bulldog, but they also address emotional and behavioral aspects. These regular visits offer an opportunity to detect any problems at an early stage, provide appropriate treatment, and ensure a long and happy life for our beloved furry companions. Don't forget to schedule your next vet appointment, your Bulldog will thank you!

Chapter 16: French Bulldog and its longevity

Explore the factors that can influence the French Bulldog's longevity and discover how to provide them with a healthy and fulfilling life to increase their life expectancy.

The French Bulldog is a dog breed as peculiar as it is charming. His rugged appearance, his big ears, and his friendly personality make him one of the most loved companions by pet owners. However, it's important to understand that this adorable breed can also face some challenges in terms of its health and longevity.

The longevity of a French Bulldog can vary depending on several factors. One of the determining aspects is genetics. As with any other dog breed, some French Bulldogs can inherit genetic predisposition to certain diseases. Respiratory, heart, or dermatological problems can affect the quality of life and life expectancy of these dogs. For this reason, it's essential to get your French Bulldog from a reputable breeder who has performed genetic testing on its parents to rule out possible hereditary problems.

In addition to genetic factors, there are other important variables that can influence the longevity of this fascinating breed. Food is one of the fundamental pillars for providing a healthy and long life for your French Bulldog. A balanced diet, appropriate to your needs, rich in essential nutrients, can help strengthen your immune system and prevent diseases. Consult your veterinarian for specific recommendations on feeding and weight management for your pet.

Regular exercise is also key to keeping your French Bulldog in optimal physical and mental condition. Although they may seem lazy, these dogs need daily activity to avoid overweight problems and to stimulate their minds. Walks, interactive games and activities that test their cunning are great for keeping them fit and happy. Remember to adapt the level of exercise to your pet's age and state of health to avoid unnecessary injuries.

In addition to adequate nutrition and exercise, taking care of your French Bulldog's oral health is an essential aspect of their longevity. This breed is prone to dental problems due to its compact facial structure. Plaque formation and tartar build-up can lead to periodontal diseases that affect your overall well-being. Establishing a regular toothbrushing routine and scheduling regular visits to the vet for professional oral cleaning are key preventive measures.

In short, if you want to ensure a healthy and full life for your French Bulldog, you need to consider a number of fundamental aspects. Genetics, diet, exercise and dental care are some of the factors that can influence your longevity. Always remember to provide him with adequate veterinary care and to act in a preventive manner to identify and treat any health problems in a timely manner.

Don't miss the second part of this chapter in which we'll explore other determining factors to increase the life expectancy of your French Bulldog. Discover how the environment, emotional enrichment and comprehensive care can be key to your adorable companion enjoying a long and happy life. The environment in which your French Bulldog lives also plays an important role in their longevity and well-being. Just like any other pet, these dogs need a safe and stimulating environment to stay happy and healthy. Make sure you provide them with a quiet and comfortable place to rest, as well as an adequate space to play and explore. It's also important to avoid excessive exposure to extreme heat or cold, as French Bulldogs are sensitive to high and low temperatures.

Emotional enrichment is another crucial factor in increasing your French Bulldog's life expectancy. These dogs are very loyal and need to be close to their owners to feel safe and loved. Spend quality time interacting with your pet, providing care, love, and mind-stimulating activities. Toy-finding games, dog puzzles, and training sessions are great ways to keep your French Bulldog mentally active and satisfied.

In addition to the environment and emotional enrichment, comprehensive health care is essential to prolong the life of your French Bulldog. Schedule regular visits to the vet for health checks, vaccinations, deworming and any other necessary preventive care. It's also important to watch for possible signs of illness or discomfort in your pet, such as changes in appetite, activity, or behavior. If you have any worrying symptoms, do not hesitate to see your veterinarian immediately.

Last but not least, love and commitment are critical to ensuring a long and happy life for your French Bulldog. These dogs become members of the family and need to feel valued and loved. Give your pet the attention and dedication they deserve, providing them with a safe home, adequate food, regular exercise and health care. The unconditional love you offer your French Bulldog will be repaid with years of company, joy and loyalty.

In conclusion, the longevity of the French Bulldog can be influenced by several factors, and there are steps you can take as an owner to increase their life expectancy. Providing him with a healthy diet, exercising regularly, taking care of his oral health, providing a stimulating environment, enriching him emotionally and offering him comprehensive care are some of the ways you can contribute to the well-being and longevity of your adorable companion. Always remember to seek the guidance of a veterinarian and act proactively to keep your French Bulldog in optimal condition. Enjoy the wonderful experience of sharing your life with this fascinating and charming breed!

Chapter 17: French Bulldog and its relationship with the owners

It analyzes the close emotional and emotional relationship that forms between French Bulldogs and their owners, and how this affects their well-being and happiness.

French Bulldogs are known for their charming and friendly personalities, making them loyal and beloved companions for their owners. The close emotional connection between French Bulldogs and their owners is something truly special. These adorable dogs have the ability to make their owners fall in love with their unique character and unconditional loyalty.

The relationship between a French Bulldog and its owner is often described as a deep connection. These dogs quickly become an integral part of the family, and their owners regard them as true-life partners. The love and devotion that French Bulldogs show to their owners is evident in every gesture and look.

One of the most fascinating aspects of this relationship is the impact it has on the dog's well-being and happiness. French Bulldogs need a strong emotional connection with their owners to feel safe and satisfied. The lack of attention and affection can lead the bulldog to experience anxiety and stress, negatively affecting their quality of life.

It is important to note that French Bulldogs are sensitive and emotional dogs. They need the company and love of their owners to develop a balanced and happy personality. Daily interaction, games, and displays of affection are crucial to your emotional well-being.

The relationship between the French Bulldog and its owner also plays a fundamental role in its behavior. When they feel loved and safe, these dogs are more likely to show calm and balanced behavior. On the other hand, inattention can lead to problematic behaviors such as destructiveness or aggressiveness.

Communication between the French Bulldog and its owner is another essential aspect of this relationship. These dogs have an innate ability to understand and respond to human emotions. They can sense if their owner is sad or happy, and act accordingly. This unique emotional connection is what makes French Bulldogs so special and loved.

The close relationship between French Bulldogs and their owners also has a positive impact on the health of both. Numerous studies have shown that the presence of a loving pet reduces stress and blood pressure for their owners. In addition, French Bulldogs are known for their ability to lift spirits and bring joy to those around them.

In short, the close emotional and affective relationship between French Bulldogs and their owners is something truly extraordinary. These adorable dogs become part of the family and their presence is essential to their well-being and happiness. The deep connection between the French Bulldog and its owner is a relationship based on love, loyalty and companionship, which has a positive effect on both the dog and its owner.

The close emotional and affective relationship between French Bulldogs and their owners is so deep and special that it goes beyond simple pets. These adorable dogs become loyal and beloved companions, capable of providing unconditional love and a unique connection with their owners.

One of the most moving aspects of this relationship is the ability of French Bulldogs to read and respond to the emotions of their owners. These sensitive and intuitive dogs are able to detect if their owner is going through moments of sadness or anxiety, and they will do their best to provide comfort and support. It's amazing how they can offer a sweet and affectionate look, or simply cuddle up with their owner to convey calm and tranquility.

The presence of a French Bulldog can have an enormous impact on the emotional well-being of its owners. The simple act of petting your furry friend can release endorphins, the "hormones of happiness," and reduce anxiety and stress. In addition, sharing quality time with the French Bulldog can improve mood and strengthen the emotional bond between the owner and the pet.

Another fascinating aspect of this relationship is how French Bulldogs can be a constant source of joy and fun. With their playful and energetic personality, they are always willing to participate in games and tricks. Whether they're chasing a ball, jumping and running in the park, or just enjoying a good time of cuddling and tickling, French Bulldogs know how to brighten up their owners' day.

In addition, the constant companionship of a French Bulldog can be especially beneficial for those who live alone or face difficult situations. These tender and loyal dogs are capable of providing a sense of companionship and protection that can fill emotional gaps and offer invaluable support.

It is important to note that the relationship between a French Bulldog and its owner must be based on respect and mutual responsibility. French Bulldogs require constant care and attention, just like any other pet. It is vital to provide them with good nutrition, adequate exercise and to meet their medical needs to ensure their physical and emotional well-being.

In addition, love and dedication should not be limited only to moments of play and affection. French Bulldogs must be educated in a positive and supportive environment, using training techniques based on positive reinforcement. This will help them to develop a balanced and pleasant behavior, and to further strengthen the special bond with their owners.

In conclusion, the close relationship between French Bulldogs and their owners is a source of happiness and well-being for both parties. These charming and affectionate dogs become true life partners, providing unconditional love, emotional support and constant fun. The deep and special connection that forms between a French Bulldog and its owner is an invaluable treasure that deserves to be protected and cultivated.

Chapter 18: French Bulldog and Stress

Understand how the French Bulldog can experience stress and anxiety, and discover effective techniques to help him manage these negative emotions.

The French Bulldog is a breed that is as charming as it is peculiar. Their unique physical features and sympathetic personality are undoubtedly part of their attraction. However, like any living being, French bulldogs can also experience stress and anxiety in certain situations. It's important that the owners of these adorable pets understand how to identify and manage these negative emotions to ensure their well-being.

Stress in dogs can manifest itself in a variety of ways: changes in behavior, agitation, excessive barking, lack of appetite, among others. In the particular case of French bulldogs, their sensitive and emotional nature can make them more likely to experience these reactions when faced with challenging or stressful situations. It is essential to identify the causes that trigger stress in our beloved furry companions.

One of the most common stressors for French bulldogs is separation from their owners. These dogs are known for their strong attachment to their families and can become anxious and stressed when left alone for extended periods. The change of environment can also be stressful for them, especially when they are in unfamiliar places. It's important to consider these situations and provide them with the support and security they need.

How can we help our French bulldogs manage stress and anxiety? There are several effective techniques that can make a difference in your emotional well-being. First, it's essential to establish a daily routine that offers them structure and stability. French bulldogs feel more secure when they know what to expect, so maintaining regular schedules for eating, exercising, and resting can help reduce their stress level.

Socialization also plays a crucial role in stress management in French bulldogs. Gradually exposing them to different people, animals and environments from an early age allows them to develop adaptive skills and gives them tools to face new situations. In addition, obedience training can be beneficial, as it provides them with a solid foundation of trust and teaches them to respond appropriately in different circumstances.

Another effective technique for reducing stress in French bulldogs is the use of relaxation methods, such as mental stimulation, quiet play and gentle massage sessions. These activities help them to clear their minds and release accumulated tensions. In addition, it is important to create a comfortable physical environment free from stressful stimuli, ensuring that they have their own quiet and safe space where they can retire when they need it.

In short, French bulldogs are adorably special, but they can also experience stress and anxiety just like other breeds. As responsible owners, it's our job to understand and address these emotional needs. By identifying the causes of stress and implementing effective techniques, we can provide them with the support they need to enjoy a full and happy life, free from the emotional burdens that stress can cause.

In the second half of this chapter, we'll delve into additional techniques to help French bulldogs manage stress effectively and ensure their emotional well-being.

One of the useful strategies for reducing stress in French bulldogs is environmental enrichment. These dogs are intelligent and need mental stimulation to stay happy and balanced. Providing them with interactive toys, puzzles for dogs and activities that challenge their mind will help reduce their stress level. In addition, regular exercise is essential to release accumulated tensions and promote mental peace of mind. Daily walks, play in the park, and other physical activities will provide a healthy outlet for channeling their energy and strengthening their emotional well-being.

Another important aspect to consider is proper nutrition. Diet plays a crucial role in the mental health of French bulldogs. Some foods can affect your mood and stress level. It is advisable to talk to your veterinarian to establish a balanced diet appropriate to the needs of your French bulldog. A balanced diet, rich in essential nutrients, can help reduce your stress and maintain good overall health.

In addition, it is important to avoid physical or verbal punishment as a method of correction. French bulldogs are especially sensitive and will respond better to positive reinforcement techniques. Using rewards, praise, and caresses when they perform a desired behavior will help them associate positive experiences with situations that might have caused them stress before.

Communication and patience are essential in the relationship with our French bulldogs. We must learn to read their signs of stress and anxiety, such as licking their lips, yawning, or hiding, so that we can intervene in time and provide them with the support they need. Speaking in a calm, reassuring tone can be comforting for them.

It's also important to remember that every French bulldog is unique and may respond differently to stress management techniques. Sometimes, it may be necessary to seek the help of a professional, such as a dog trainer or a veterinarian specializing in animal behavior, who can provide personalized and more specialized advice.

In conclusion, understanding and managing stress in French bulldogs is essential to ensure their well-being and happiness. Through effective techniques such as establishing routines, socialization, environmental enrichment, proper nutrition, and empathetic communication, we can help our adorable companions to deal with stressful situations in a healthier way. Remember that caring for our pets is an ongoing responsibility, and being willing to adapt to their emotional needs is an integral part of this relationship.

Chapter 19: Legends and curiosities about the French Bulldog

Immerse yourself in the fascinating legends and curiosities surrounding the French Bulldog, from its presence in popular culture to peculiar myths and beliefs.

The French Bulldog is a dog breed that has captured the hearts of many people around the world. His unique appearance and charming personality have made him one of the most popular and loved dogs. However, behind this fascinating breed, there are legends and curiosities that never cease to surprise.

One of the best-known legends about the French Bulldog is its supposed connection to the world of magic. These dogs are said to have special powers and are capable of detecting negative energies. French Bulldog owners claim that their pets are excellent home protectors and can ward off any type of evil entity. This belief has led some people to consider the French Bulldog as a good luck and protection charm.

Another curiosity surrounding this breed is its presence in the world of art and popular culture. The French Bulldog has been represented in paintings, movies and even in fashion. Their peculiar figure and unique expression have been captured by artists who seek to convey the essence and beauty of these adorable dogs. In addition, the popularity of this breed has led famous people such as musicians, actors and athletes to become proud owners of the French Bulldog, which has contributed to its iconic image in contemporary culture.

However, there are also peculiar myths and beliefs surrounding the French Bulldog. One of them is that these dogs are protective by nature and can become aggressive. However, the owners and experts on the breed claim quite the opposite. The French Bulldog is characterized by being a friendly, gentle and sociable dog. His charming personality and his unconditional affection for his owners are traits that have made him an ideal companion for many people.

In addition, it has been mentioned that French Bulldogs have a special ability to perceive the emotions of their owners. They are said to be able to detect when someone is sad, in need of company or in danger. This emotional sensitivity has made them considered therapy dogs in some cases, being able to provide support and comfort to people who are going through difficult times.

These peculiarities and mysteries surrounding the French Bulldog make this breed one of the most interesting and captivating. Its presence in popular culture, it's supposed magical powers and its capacity for emotional connection with humans have amazed many. But this is only the first part of the story, because there is still more to discover and explore about the secrets and charms of the French Bulldog.

Eager to learn more about this exciting breed, we will enter the second half of this chapter, where we will discover more legends and curiosities. Get ready to dive even deeper into the fascinating world of the French Bulldog and its charming personality. The adventure continues!

The French Bulldog continues to surprise with its charm and mystery, and in the second half of this chapter we will explore more legends and curiosities surrounding this fascinating dog breed.

A curiosity that cannot go unnoticed is the connection between the French Bulldog and fashion. These adorable dogs have been protagonists on the most important catwalks and have captured the hearts of renowned designers. Their peculiar figure and unique expression have inspired the creation of clothing and accessories, turning them into true icons of style. Some French Bulldogs have even had the opportunity to walk the runways with famous models, leaving tenderness and elegance in their wake.

But not only does this breed stand out in fashion, it has also left its mark in the sports field. Many French Bulldogs have been companions to high-performance athletes, witnessing their training and competitions. These dogs, with their energy and enthusiasm, have served as motivation and support for athletes from different disciplines. They are loyal companions who are always willing to cheer and provide affection, a true source of inspiration in the world of sport.

Among the most peculiar legends surrounding the French Bulldog, is the belief that these dogs have the ability to predict the weather. Some owners claim that their dogs show unusual behavior just before a change in atmospheric conditions occurs, such as changes in wind or atmospheric pressure. Although there is no scientific evidence to support this statement, it is curious how these beliefs are transmitted from generation to generation, adding a touch of mystery to this peculiar breed.

Another fascinating feature of French Bulldogs is their ability to adapt. Despite their robust appearance, they are ideal dogs for living in small spaces such as apartments. Their easy-going personality and need for company make them perfect companions for people who don't have a large outdoor space. In addition, their low level of physical activity makes them adapt to more sedentary lifestyles, as long as they are provided with the necessary care to maintain their health.

These are just some of the many curiosities surrounding the French Bulldog, a breed that continues to captivate and amaze all those who are fortunate to have them as life partners. Their charm, charming personality and unique peculiarities make them adorable and special dogs.

This is how we ended the second half of this chapter, but the story of the French Bulldog continues. Soon, you'll have the opportunity to continue exploring and discovering more secrets and peculiarities surrounding this fascinating breed. Get ready to dive even deeper into the adventure of meeting the French Bulldog and his charming personality!

Chapter 20: Adoption and Rescue of French Bulldogs

Learn how you can be part of the noble task of giving a home to abandoned or endangered French Bulldogs.

Adopting a French Bulldog is a rewarding experience for both the new owner and the dog. Through adoption, a second chance is given to these wonderful animals that have suffered abandonment or neglect by their former owners. In addition, it is a way to help alleviate the overpopulation of dogs in shelters and promote the protection of this charming breed.

When you decide to adopt a French Bulldog, you're taking a courageous and generous step. These dogs have a lot of love and gratitude to offer, despite the difficulties they have faced in the past. However, before venturing into the adoption process, it's crucial that you are aware of what it entails and prepare yourself properly for this great responsibility.

The first step is to research and find shelters or organizations dedicated to the rescue of French Bulldogs in your area. These places are responsible for providing temporary shelter, veterinary care and rehabilitation for rescued dogs, until they find a permanent home. You can search online or consult with veterinarians and animal lovers in your community, who can guide you through the adoption process.

Once you've identified a reliable shelter or organization, it's important to visit it to meet the French Bulldogs available for adoption. You will have the opportunity to interact with them and assess if there is a connection and compatibility between you and the dog. Remember that every French Bulldog has a unique personality and it's essential that you find the dog that best fits your lifestyle and needs.

During your visit to the shelter, it's critical to ask questions and get information about the medical and behavioral history of the dog you're considering adopting. Make sure the dog has received the necessary veterinary care and has been evaluated by canine behavior experts. This will help you make an informed decision and ensure that you can provide a safe and suitable environment for the dog once they arrive at their new home.

In addition, it's important to note that adopting a French Bulldog can require an investment of time and resources. These dogs may need additional training, socialization, and special care because of their previous history. Get ready to be committed to working on their well-being and providing them with the love and attention they deserve.

In short, the adoption and rescue of French Bulldogs is an opportunity to make a difference in the lives of these wonderful dogs. By opening your home and heart to a rescued French Bulldog, you will be providing a new opportunity for happiness and love to a being in desperate need. Remember, by adopting, you are saving a life and building a special relationship that will last forever.

Continue... By making the decision to adopt a rescued French Bulldog, you are opening the doors of your home to a being in desperate need of a second chance. However, it's important to note that adopting a rescue dog can take time, patience, and dedication. In this second half of the chapter, we'll explore more key aspects to consider before bringing your new furry companion home.

Once you've committed to adopting a rescued French Bulldog, it's essential to prepare your home to receive it in the best possible way. Make sure you have a safe and adequate space for the dog, with all the necessary amenities, such as a comfortable bed, fresh water and appropriate toys. In addition, it is essential to make sure that your home is free from potential hazards, such as toxic plants or chemicals within reach of the dog.

The next step is to adjust your expectations and understand that each rescued French Bulldog will have its own adaptation process. The dog is likely to have experienced traumatic experiences in the past, which can affect his behavior and confidence level. Be patient and give him the time and space he needs to feel safe and comfortable in his new environment.

For the first few weeks, it's a good idea to establish a daily routine for your rescued dog. This will provide you with security and structure, which will contribute to your emotional well-being. Make sure you dedicate time to exercising and socializing your dog every day, as he gets used to his new home and environment.

In addition, it is crucial to have the support of a trusted veterinarian to ensure the health and well-being of your rescued French Bulldog. Schedule an initial visit so the vet can perform a complete checkup and assess any specific medical needs your dog may have. Be sure to follow veterinary recommendations regarding vaccines, deworming and proper diet to the letter.

Patience and consistency are key to the adaptation process of a rescued dog. You may face challenges during this time, such as behavioral problems or difficulties in establishing the relationship between you and the dog. In such cases, consider seeking guidance from a dog trainer or participating in socialization classes for dogs. These professionals can provide you with tools and advice to help you establish a healthy and nurturing relationship with your new furry companion.

Don't forget to celebrate small achievements as your rescued French Bulldog progresses through its adaptation process. Every moment of trust, every line moving and every bark of joy are signs that you are playing a key role in the life of this wonderful being.

In conclusion, the adoption and rescue of French Bulldogs is a rewarding experience that requires significant personal investment. By providing a loving and safe home to a rescued French Bulldog, you'll be making a difference in their life and building a special bond that will last forever. Remember, dogs have incredible potential to heal and love, and you can be that person who gives them a second chance. Adopt and change a life forever!

Disclaimer

The information provided in this book is for general informational and educational purposes only and is not intended as a substitute for professional advice, diagnosis, or treatment. The author and publisher have made every effort to ensure the accuracy and reliability of the information provided within these pages, but they make no guarantees, either express or implied, regarding the content's completeness, accuracy, or applicability.

Neither the author nor the publisher shall be held liable or responsible for any misunderstanding or misuse of the information contained in this book or for any loss, damage, or injury caused, or alleged to be caused, directly or indirectly by any treatment, action, or application of any advice discussed in this publication. The statements made within this book are not intended to diagnose, treat, cure, or prevent any disease. Readers should consult with a qualified healthcare provider for medical advice tailored to their personal circumstances.

The views and opinions expressed herein are those of the author alone and do not necessarily reflect the official policy or position of any agency or company. All content provided in this book is on an "as-is" basis and the author and publisher disclaim all responsibility for any errors or omissions.

Also by Gonzalo Estrada

Self Healing
Visualiza tu Éxito
Cultivando Líderes
Afirmaciones y Empoderamiento
Semillas de Cambio
Cómo convertir TikTok en una máquina de hacer dinero
Cómo hacer dinero con Pinterest
Cómo hacer un ensayo
Cómo Pedir un Aumento de Sueldo
Currículo Poderoso
Entrenamiento sin Violencia
Entrevista Laboral
Gana Dinero con X (Twitter)
Ganar Masa Muscular
Volver a Empezar; el arte de reinventarse
Analiza Resuelve Ejecuta
Aromatherapy, The natural path to your pet´s well being
Holistic Feeding
The ABC of Educating Your Pet
The Art of Cosmic Connection
The Art of Feng Shui applied to your Pets
From Scarcity to Abundance
The English Bulldog in The Family
The French Bulldog
Therapeutic Massages for Pets